Children's Book about Germany

Germania and the Roman Empire

Children's Ancient History Books

Left Brain Kids

Educational Books for Children

A long time ago,
Germania was under the
conquest of the Roman Empire.

Let's learn about Germania and how it gained independence from the Romans!

Germania was a term used by the Romans and Greeks for a region that was mainly inhabited by Germanic people.

Germania covered a land area of 190, 000 square miles and as of the first century BC, it was inhabited by 5,000,000 people.

The country has three rivers along its borders. To the west is the Rhine River; to the south, the Danube River; and to the east, the Vistula River.

During the first century BC, the areas west of the Rhine River were mostly Celtic but were under the Roman Empire.

The people who inhabited Germania were Germanic, Celtic, Scynthian, Baltic and Proto-Slavic.

They spoke different dialects. So to somehow unite the people, two main tribes were established.

The first was called the Lesser Germania, and was composed of tribes under the Roman Empire.

The second was
called the Greater
Germania, and
was composed
of tribes outside
the control of the
Roman Empire.

Over time, the country's ethnic and tribal makeup changed due to migration.

Julius Caesar had described the differences of culture between the Germanic tribesmen, the Gauls, and the Romans. He noted that although Gauls were warlike, they could also be civilized.

On the other hand, he saw that the Germanic tribesmen were very savage so they were considered great threats to the Roman Gauls. Because of this, the Germanic tribesmen had to be conquered.

In 12 BC and under the command of Augustus, with Legati Generals Tiberius and Germanicus leading their legions, Romans began to conquer and defeat the peoples in Germania Magna.

In 6 AD, Romans ruled and temporarily pacified all of Germania, including those who settled along the River Elbe.

In 9 AD, the Roman's plan to conquer all of Magna Germania failed because the German tribesmen fought back and defeated them in what is called the Battle of the Teutonburg Forest.

Augustus had to order the Romans to retreat from Magna Germania and the Roman Empire had to establish their boundaries somewhere else, along the Rhine and Danube.

It is evident that the Roman Empire had exercised great power and control over its neighboring territories. But the Germanic tribes fought back and ultimately regained their freedom.

If you want to read more about the Germania, then the Tacitus' Germania will be another great resource!